Traver, Hope
Allegory and Mysticism
in Shakespeare

Allegory and Mysticism in Shakespeare

J. Russell & Sons Ltd. photographers — Emery Walker Ltd. ph. x.

Allegory and Mysticism in Shakespeare

A Medievalist on
"The Merchant of Venice"

Reports of three Lectures by

Sir Israel Gollancz

In Memoriam

Printed for Private Circulation by GEO. W. JONES at *The Sign of The Dolphin* in Gough Square, London
June, 1931

To
His Friends and Colleagues

Alide Gollancz

To a Fellow-Mourner

A sullen sea, and dark the hórizon,
And footsore by the strand a lonely wight.
But yesterday the waters gleam'd with light,
The limitless with buoyant radiance shone.
On this shore wander we, beloved friend;
The severing Ocean and the flinty strands
Part those we fain would grasp with loving hands;
Our joyous yesterdays too soon have end.
The weather-wise peer through the dark'ning sky,
And "all is well," say they, on yonder shore;
The light is theirs that fadeth nevermore—
Wisdom 'bove human Knowledge soaring high.
    They know how human Love can never cease;
    We know, as they, that perfect Love is Peace.

I. G.

Preface

SIR ISRAEL GOLLANCZ edited many texts and wrote many prefaces,
but he preferred speaking to writing, and amid the mass of papers
which he left there was none which bore evidence of having been
prepared or intended to be printed. The subject treated, from
slightly different angles, in these three lectures, was one of his favourite topics, and as these short-hand notes were in existence, Lady
Gollancz thought that his friends would be glad to have copies
of them, while understanding that he himself would never have
~~their present~~ form. Sincere thanks are due
~~Dr. Hope Traver for the care~~ with which she has revised these
reports in order to eliminate the errors of hearing, and supply, here
and there, a word dropped out in the transcript. For some further
touchings Dr. Mabel Day and the present writer must take respon-
sibility, but there are still several passages where one or more words
seem to conflict with the general sense, and which yet could not
be emended with any safety. The roughness, even an occasional
incoherence, will be forgiven by those who can catch in these un-
studied deliverances the tones of Sir Israel's voice and his eagerness
in speaking on a favourite theme. Any more drastic editing would
almost certainly have diminished the sense of his present personality which, at least to some who have read them, the papers in

Edited by

Dr. Hope Traver

Dept. of English)

Mills College

their present form convey. The task which the speaker essayed was the hazardous one of trying to suggest what Shakespeare had not only in his conscious, but in his subconscious mind, and complete success was impossible. It is the more interesting to note the fascination which it exercised, so that it was essayed again and again. Those who care for Israel Gollancz, as well as those who care for William Shakespeare, may find that, as to the one no less than as to the other, something is here suggested to them which they had not suspected.

ALFRED W. POLLARD

Thanks are offered to Messrs. J. Russell & Sons, 63 Baker Street, W., for leave to reproduce the photograph of Sir Israel Gollancz.

The "Shylock" of Shakespeare

*Lecture delivered before the Jewish Historical Society
at University College, Gower Street, W.C.
Monday, 22nd May, 1916*

Mr. President, Ladies and Gentlemen—I am not this evening
going to put before you all those different variations of the Shylock
story that are to be found in all the different nations East and West.
A whole volume might easily be made up of the variations of the
theme familiar to us—we will take that as understood by all of
you—and in almost every country of Europe these stories are to be
found. I am not even going to point out the varyings of the Shylock
story in which the villain of the piece, the Shylock, is not the Jew
but the non-Jew. All that, we will take as readily known to every-
one in the room. No edition of Shakespeare's play is without an
introduction setting forth the stories that Shakespeare used or is
supposed to have used, or setting forth all the knowledge that the
editor happens to possess of parallels to the Shylock story. I am not
going to deal with the play or the character from that point of
view. What I am going to try to do is this : I am going to take, as
it were, an entirely fresh perspective of the play in its relation to
literature and to drama. I am not going to hold any brief for
Shakespeare's humanity or for his attempt to satisfy the prejudices
of his age. I am simply going to put the character of the whole play

in a position that I think may quicken apprehension of what is at the back of the play, and help to an understanding of what belongs to the theme as its inherent intrinsic part of the plot that Shakespeare took over, whatever he may have made of it. Now what I am becoming more and more impressed with as I attempt to understand Shakespeare is this: that Shakespeare, as is the case with many of the very greatest artists, whether they be poets or whether they be dramatists, or whether they belong to the plastic arts or the art of painting, that Shakespeare, in dealing with each of his stories, with the tale or the novel or whatever else might have come to his hand, had the instinctive power of divining—unconsciously perchance, but divining—the germ of the particular myth behind it. I mean this: if you take such a play as *King Lear* you have a story there of an ancient king of Britain who, in his old age, became very foolish in his attitude towards his children, and who suffers tribulation from the two daughters who are cruel and heartless, and who finds the comfort that he had originally rejected from the gentle daughter Cordelia. We know the play, we know how difficult it is to put on the stage, we know how any representation of it is a vain attempt to do justice to the drama. You turn to your critics and your critics tell you this or that should be the characteristic of the actor performing Lear or the daughters; and then comes a great critic, such as Charles Lamb, who, going to the play and seeing some of the greatest performers perform Lear, boldly writes that "the Lear of Shakespeare cannot be acted." And yet Shakespeare wrote his play for acting, and Charles Lamb was no mean critic, and Shakespeare was no mean dramatist. Then in course of time comes the student of early British history, and he

14

makes an interesting discovery; he discovers that it is true. In British history you come across the story of King Lear, you know the date when he reigned, you know everything about him—is he not in history books? Then comes your student of folk-lore and anthropology, and makes it clear that the history we have of King Lear in history books represents the rationalisation of an ancient myth, where King Lear is Neptune, the Scandinavian and Celtic Neptune, and the rough, heartless daughters are the fierce waves, and the gentle Cordelia is the mild wave. Shakespeare knows nothing concerning what is at the back of this myth which figures in British history, which dramatists before him had found a delightful theme for entrancing Elizabethan audiences. He knows nothing of that, but his genius unconsciously divines the myth, and so the Lear of Shakespeare becomes something too great for any stage.

I shall not trouble you with history, though you are the Jewish Historical Society. If you look at this play of *The Merchant of Venice* carefully you will have to consider at what point it comes into the whole range of drama, that Elizabethan drama which, during its first thirty years, from about 1558 to 1588, had all the elements, commingling elements, linking that Elizabethan age far back to the very beginning of the Christian Church on the one hand and, on the other, ranging far back to a period long before the beginning of Christianity, to the ancient drama of Greece and Rome. All these elements are commingled in that period of formation of the Elizabethan drama from 1558 to 1588. And, in the long procession that one sees, a long-drawn-out procession heralding Shakespeare, one may, in fact, in that rapid, moving procession see one or two important items to which, very briefly, I desire to draw your attention.

You know that even in the Elizabethan Age we still had the old drama existing, going back to the time when the Christian Church, by creating a Liturgical drama, tried to win the newly converted pagans from the attractions of the gladiatorial shows. The Church found that the best way to do that was to dramatise, first, the Offices of the Church and, secondly, Bible stories; and in our procession of the new drama, the drama of the modern world, that dramatising of the Scriptural stories takes a very important place. The Church learnt very early that in order to teach the people, an illiterate people, the best way was to appeal to them through the pageants of the Liturgical drama and the whole history of the Bible from creation to the crack of doom. All sorts of elements were introduced and were very early dramatised. But, very early, I should think probably between the eighth and tenth centuries of the Christian era, there was discovered a very obvious thing, namely, that not only was it desirable to teach the people the Biblical story by dramatising that story, but that you might appeal to the congregation by dramatising a Scriptural text— practically the sermon dramatised. And that brings us to the second stage in the history of our modern drama: this early medieval drama, the dramatisation of the Scriptural text. Already about the twelfth century we have such a theme as "Righteousness and peace have kissed one another." It took some three centuries before this kind of drama, the moral drama in which the characters were allegorical and set forth for the education and betterment of human life, became a popular form of drama in England. We have it by the fifteenth century. This was a drama of allegory, and were my theme allegory I could very well give the minutes at my disposal to dealing with that subject alone.

Its importance is not well recognised. Allegory was made an important point of interpretation of Biblical texts by the early Church Fathers. But allegory became predominant in English literature from the fourteenth to the fifteenth century; and anyway, in Shakespeare's early youth he not only beheld from the pageants, such as he saw in Coventry, the story of Noah, the story of Jacob, of Abraham and Isaac, but he also saw sermons, moral plays put before him. And we know of one contemporary, a young boy of Gloucester born in the same year, who left us an account, some years after Shakespeare's death, how, as a child, standing between his father's knees, he beheld one of these moral plays, *The Cradle of Security,* and how the influence of this play in which all the characters were allegorical remained an abiding possession throughout his whole life.

Now, if there is one subject that interested the early Churchmen in preaching their sermons it was, of course, the great story, the essential part of the Christian creed. Let us approach it as students, and see what would happen supposing a preacher of the eleventh or twelfth century were to put effectively and dramatically before a crude and rude audience such a text as the following: "Greater love hath no man than this, that a man should lay down his life for his friend," or such a text as this: "Christ also loved the Church and gave Himself for it." No text was more often used by the preachers, and if you attempt to put before an unlettered audience either of these texts or both of them, you will have a

Moral drama enforcing the lesson that the preacher wished to enforce. How else is it to be done save by showing in contrast the tenderness and self-sacrifice of Christ on the one hand and the alleged heartlessness, the alleged brutality, according to the popular traditional hatred and bias, of the Jew on the other hand? And if, when you have put these two characters in juxtaposition for the purpose of enforcing the text, you wish to graft on to that one text the second text that I have quoted, "Christ also loved the Church and gave Himself for it," how else is your Church to be personified save as the spouse desired and longed for?

So that your second text must needs provide not only the lady typifying salvation, tenderness, the fairest attribute of the Almighty —not only that, but also a sequence of suitors who, in order to win her, make their various efforts, and for whom, as regards the one particular suitor who is to succeed, the self-sacrificing character is ready to give his very life-blood, his very heart, to the cruel adversary typifying the attribute of cruelty associated in the popular mind with our own people. Now, you will say that I cannot point to chapter or verse for such an explanation at the back of the Shylock story; but read your medieval literature, such a book for example as *The Nuns' Rule,* which belongs to about the early thirteenth century, one of the most beautiful books in English literature, written by a man who understood human nature, and especially the nature of the nuns he wrote for. In that book we have these texts, both these texts, chosen and allegorised in a very fine way so that the lady, the spouse, the Church, becomes a noble lady who is besieged in her castle by many an adversary until at last the right wooer, the son of a neighbouring king, is victorious, and in that book, which belonged to the thirteenth century, we come across the following reference : "Do not men account him a good friend who layeth his pledge in Jewry to release his companion." "God Almighty laid Himself in Jewry for us."

I therefore say that the starting-point of the legend of Shylock —I would insist on emphasising it as the legend, the legend going back to the time of prejudice and hatred which can still be understood—that legend had been created, I feel sure, by some early monkish divine in a dramatic homily, and from that dramatic homily all the permutations and combinations have developed. And I will say this, that when, in the text-books and studies which we constantly have of *The Merchant of Venice,* we are told that the story of Shylock comes from one particular source and the story of the Fair Lady of Belmont from another source—all that is, to my mind, quite fictitious. There may be different variants with reference to the two component parts of the story, but they represent the component parts of one and the same story arising out of the blending of the two texts I have quoted to you.

By about the middle of the sixteenth century the Moral drama in England was becoming obsolete, but was still co-existing side by side with other forms of drama. Shakespeare knew this form of drama—the Moral drama—and when he was a boy (I am talking of 1574 to 1579, when he was quite a lad), in the year 1579 already in London a play was performed in which the two component parts (the play is lost now, we only know it from reference) were the bloody minds of usurers and the greed of worldly choosers, that is, both the story of Shylock and the story of the Caskets. That has disappeared, but I am inclined to think that

that play was very near indeed to the Moral drama. A corresponding play that does exist called *The Three Ladies of London* gives us elements so near to the allegorical Moral drama that I have mentioned, as to give us almost a conviction that even if the characters in the play mentioned in 1579 were all real, the names were rather nicknames than real personages and characters.

That brings us to about 1579, that is, when Shakespeare was fifteen, when the subject, as we have it referred to in *The Merchant of Venice,* had already been dramatised. We cannot point to the positive source that the author of the play had used. This is of minor consequence. The point is that it represents a play dealing with a problem the Elizabethans were very much interested in, namely, the problem of usury. And it is with that problem in view that right through the Elizabethan Age we have a series of pamphlets at a time when there were practically no Jews in England. The Jewish question had nothing to do with that problem which was the great problem of the Church, a social and ecclesiastical problem—the problem of usury. This man, in 1579, took the whole legend and dealt with it in so expressive and dramatic a way that it received praise from Stephen Gosson (who disapproved plays generally), a Puritan preacher.

Then we come to the period when Shakespeare was being heralded by a whole group of great men, a group of great poets, and the greatest of them Christopher Marlowe. He comes before us with so much ado, so much excitement and applause, that for a moment it looks as though the Master himself had come and not the herald. Very often it is so in real life. The Master comes without ostentation and the herald receives the applause.

Now about 1590 or 1591 Christopher Marlowe looked about for a theme, and found one well suited to his genius. His genius sought subjects that represented the idealisation of gigantic passion on a gigantic scale. He was a Titanic poet, and something of his neo-Titanic being he poured into the poor, lifeless vessel of the drama *Tamburlaine*. He, through sheer might and power, climbed to the very top of Fortune's Wheel, and when there thrust his fist in the face of Fortune. The steady Wheel went round, and the poor Emperor, where was he? In the pit below.

Then he chose the great theme of Dr. Faustus to idealise the passion of the lust for knowledge as opposed to wisdom—that thirst for knowledge in which

> "Our souls, whose faculties can comprehend
> The wondrous architecture of the world,
> And measure every wandering planet's course,
> Still climbing after knowledge infinite,
> And always moving as the restless spheres,
> Will us to wear ourselves, and never rest."

Then he looks round and takes the theme of the *Jew of Malta*, a theme for the lust of wealth with no idea of usury save as a passing incident associated in the popular mind with the Jewish character. The background of that play is rather the politics of the time, the problem of Turkey, the relation of the Jewish people from the Elizabethan point of view to the enemies of England— it is about 1590-91 that we have that play.

In the early part of 1593 Marlowe died, and Shakespeare, who up to that date had been, as if in awe of him, doing nothing in rivalry with Marlowe, choosing rather comedy than tragedy, for the first time comes forward as the rival of the Master, a Master born in the same year as Shakespeare himself, but yet just getting in advance of Shakespeare by a year or two, and during that year or two doing all the work necessary for the coming of the Master. He writes the play of *Richard III* on the model of Marlowe's *Tamburlaine,* he writes the play of *Richard II* on the model of Marlowe's *Edward II,* and he writes the play of *The Merchant of Venice* in rivalry, to a large extent, with Marlowe's *Jew of Malta.* He looks round for his theme. What theme was he to take? The Jew of Malta? No.

Shakespeare's interest was in Italy, there was the poet's quest—there alone were those elements in strong contrast that interested Shakespeare so much in his early work. In his early life he depicted violent love and violent hate, love as rapid as the lightning —gone before one can say "it lightens"—and hatred too. In Romeo and Juliet he had dealt with that wonderful aspect of human passion, where:

> "Two such opposed Kings encamp them still
> In man as well as herbs, grace, and rude will;
> And where the worser is predominant,
> Full soon the canker death eats up that plant."

Was it when he was thinking of Italy that he thought of the Venetian Jew? And the story which had already been localised in Venice in the same way as the story of Romeo and Juliet had been localised in Verona goes back to the time before Italy was dreamt of as a land of civilisation. He turned to Italy and no doubt he found that this Venetian Comedy would just satisfy that point of development of his genius. For a number of years, Shakespeare chose comedy pure and simple, but somewhere about 1595 to 1596 the two elements of Shakespeare's being, Comedy and Tragedy, blending in the creation of what was almost a new form in England, what might be called Tragi-Comedy sprang into life—which is not all tears, not all laughter, but a strange commingling of both. And in this play of *The Merchant of Venice* he saw his possibilities. He chose a theme which had been well known in London from its popularity in the courtyards of taverns. We come as early as 1579 on the "Bloody minds of Usurers and the greediness of worldly choosers." Now I am sure that if we were to rediscover by any chance that old play, we should be astonished to see how much of the timber of Shakespeare's play was there.

Shakespeare did not mind about conveying timber. As all men of genius know, the name is graven on the workmanship. It does not matter much about the timber, and Shakespeare, as a great artist, took timber where he saw much might be made of it, the name being graven on the workmanship, and that name being Shakespeare's. He took the old play. He worked it. It is Shakespeare.

But the first problem Shakespeare had was to find a name for his hero or his heroic villain. For to begin with, the villain of his play was to be no ideal character save ideal in villainy; he was to be the counterpart of Marlowe's Barabas, Marlowe simply giving the name which easily occurred to him to the chief character of his play. Shakespeare was careful in the choice of his names. One of the most fascinating studies in Shakespearian literature is, perhaps,

23

this investigation into the choice of names by Shakespeare. He looked round. Who was to be and what was to be the name of the hero? Now, there was one book that Elizabethans turned to when they wanted to know anything about the Jews. You say the Bible? Yes, but somehow or other the Bible did not suggest the only place where they might find them. Look at the later history of the Jews. And the most favourite book of the Elizabethan period is a book which you have often heard about in this Society, namely, Peter Morwyng's translation of the pseudo-Josephus. This was very popular. It went through edition after edition. People read it and they got all sorts of influences from it, as is seen by its influence on Marlowe's *Jew of Malta*. And now Shakespeare, reading this book, in the early part—quite in the beginning—came across a very interesting statement that when the Jews were besieged they resolved to send three of their number to go and interview a Roman General, Antonio, who was then at Askalon, and one of the chosen three within the city was Schiloch.

Schiloch is a very fascinating word about which, in a Philological Society, a great deal might be said. Shakespeare was interested in it, and seems to have appropriated it as a very good name for a Jew. But his play was to be a play on usury and one cannot emphasize enough the fact that it is, to begin with, a problem play. Now Shakespeare had an enquiring mind. He wished to give to his play a certain Biblical character, and if you read *The Merchant of Venice* you will find he gives almost a special Biblical idiom to Shylock in that he makes him speak with a twang. Not that he breathes of jargon. He speaks a very beautiful English. (Shakespeare gives this quality also to Caliban.) But there is a special idiom torn almost from the Bible that he tries to put into the lips of Shylock. As in Marlowe's *Jew of Malta* this hero-villain was to have a daughter. In Marlowe's *Jew,* the daughter's name is Abigail. Shakespeare turns to the Bible— those Bibles that in Elizabethan times and in modern times have lists of proper names with their explanations, and he finds, in this Bible, Iscah, the daughter of Haran, which means "She that looketh out." "Oh," he says, "there is what will be the name of the daughter of my hero. She, that is the daughter of the ghetto, shall pry out from the window." He sees almost visibly the elements of his plot from that, and takes the name in question. There is no doubt that Jessica was taken directly from the study of the glossary.

But what about his hero, the hero personifying the usurer? There is no question about that whatever. Other ideas there may be. I do not think anyone can doubt that in Elizabethan times the popular name for the usurer was the "Cormorant." I could quote you half a dozen passages where several or many authors used this term for usury. Indeed one man, a little later than the Elizabethan period, at the beginning of the seventeenth century, a very popular minor poet, wrote a book—a book concerning "Land Cormorants," or "Those people who feed on other people"—because the cormorant was the creature that swooped down and caught up the fishes. Now, most of you in this room know better than I do that the Hebrew for Cormorant, one of the forbidden beasts, is Shaloch, and I have not the least doubt that Shakespeare combined the Schiloch from the book already referred to with Shaloch the cormorant, and created, in the manner in which he was fond

25

of creating names, the name of his hero. Not only that. I doubt whether the name was Shylock in Elizabethan times. If you turn to an ordinary edition of Shakespeare's *Merchant of Venice* you will find the statement that Shakespeare took the name Shylock or Schiloch from a little book which appeared many years afterwards, in the seventeenth century, "Schiloch the Jew." Of course the name had been taken from Shakespeare, but it shows that the name was written Schiloch, not short, but long, as in Shylock.

Shakespeare then had his hero: the cormorant—the usurer; and, following the legend (in the same way as Chaucer in *The Prioress's Tale,* though there were no Jews in England in the fourteenth century, chose the legend of little Hugh of Lincoln and gave us the pathetic tale which jars on us but satisfies his audience—the tale of little Hugh murdered by the Jews in their Jewry), so Shakespeare took the popular legend already known, and emphasised the character of the usurer. But it was Shakespeare and not Marlowe doing the work. We see that when we compare *Richard II* with Marlowe's *Edward II,* or *Richard III* with *Tamburlaine.*

But those who read the two plays feel the difference, and so it is when one turns to Shakespeare's *Merchant of Venice.* To begin with, the theme is the theme of the usurer created with all the monstrosity and horror likely to satisfy his audience fed on the legends of the monstrosities of the Jews. But that legend had become crystallised by Shakespeare's time. Hence his rationalizing of the allegory of that text from the New Testament which I referred to; namely, his real point is that one so loves his neighbour that he is willing to give his life for him. You must, therefore, have someone who is claiming that love, claiming that heart, on the one hand, and also the friend for whom this self-sacrificing being is ready to give it. And what more natural when you know the whole development of the allegory than that the friend for whom the great sacrificer is willing to make the sacrifice wishes to woo a fair and noble lady, so noble that she can only be gained by one who, careless of the ordinary methods of the world choosing gold and silver, chooses real wealth. And the fair lady of Belmont, we can understand her ancestry; she really belongs (and Shakespeare unconsciously divines it—he does not know this but he divines it)—her pedigree links her back—to that old Midrash which passed into medieval literature, so that we have fifty or sixty variants of that old medieval Midrash, namely, Justice and Peace and Truth on the one hand and Mercy on the other. They are the four daughters. They represent your Portia, Mercy: the others are only by chance referred to. And Portia's great speech, for which so much of the great play is a preparation, represents the embodiments, as the Liturgical drama all the attributes, of the daughter of the Deity. It is as though one were listening to an old Midrash of the old allegorical form which we get in Shakespeare's own time.

I said years ago, when I did not see the force of my words (and that is the interesting part), that Portia's great speech of Mercy addressed to Shylock represents almost the epitome of a whole moral play. I am sure that in thus attempting to discover what Shakespeare himself did not understand, but what a great artist divines without understanding, I was groping towards the fact that Portia is actually Mercy personified, one of the four daughters of God, one of the four attributes of the Almighty as the old Hebrew Midrash put it.

Now people might argue and say: Yes, Shakespeare took it, but his object was to temper the prejudices of his age against the Jews; and we quote with pride, and we have quoted a great deal within the last week or two, Shakespeare's famous plea. He puts into the lips of Shylock a noble plea for tolerance, which, from that point of view, represents that power that belongs to Shakespeare of divining humanity where under ordinary conditions there might be mere monstrosity. That belongs to Shakespeare's genius, and true genius is, of course, human; but I do not go with those who would like to cut out part of the play, and say that when Shylock said that he wished the bond to be drawn up as "a merry sport," he meant it to be a merry sport, but never intended to go further—that it was only later on that he changed his mind. I do not for a moment hold with that belief. It belongs to the play, to the character, to represent Shylock as repellent, as the man willing to claim his due. But where Shakespeare cried "halt" was at this: that though this monster might, from the moment that we see him, have been willing to claim his right, yet under ordinary conditions he would have yielded to the plea for mercy. He would not have executed his diabolical revenge.

Yes, Shakespeare felt that, and yet he cannot make him change under ordinary conditions. He cannot divert him from his purpose. On the contrary the purpose has to become strengthened in Shylock. And now, in order to understand Shylock as he appeared before Elizabethan audiences, I want to introduce you to another type of drama now brought into combination. In dealing with

The Merchant of Venice, I have spoken of the allegorical drama, I have spoken of Marlowe and his drama of passion. There was, however, a kind of drama, very popular in London about 1590, a drama in which a character may become maddened by wrong, so maddened as absolutely to be willing to risk everything for the carrying out of vengeance. The best type of this drama is a play called *The Spanish Tragedy,* where a father, having lost a beloved son, Horatio (the father is called Hieronymo), seeks vengeance, and is determined to get it; becomes distraught with longing for vengeance, and ultimately becomes so keen to get it that he asks the instrument of the original wickedness to join him in the performance of a play. And that play, which is to be acted before an audience, becomes a real tragedy in which the hero in his desire for vengeance sacrifices himself, so maddened is he. "Hieronymo gone mad" became the popular theme for an Elizabethan audience.

Thus, as a great element of this play and in Shakespeare's treatment of Shylock, one must bear in mind the utmost importance of the theme of *The Spanish Tragedy.* There was an element of the comic, if one may use comedy in the deeper sense, for an Elizabethan audience to see Shylock sharpen on his shoe the knife for exacting the pound of flesh. But for the audience it was also a figure like "Hieronymo gone mad"—distraught by grief; and it was Shakespeare's great power to see by what means the distraction of Shylock, the mad determination not to give up the idea that he originally held fairly tenaciously, but would have abandoned when the plea for mercy was put before him, could be brought about.

In order to make the monstrosity of Shylock understood,

Shakespeare uses the character of Jessica—"she that looketh out from the window."

Horatio, the beloved son, murdered in *The Spanish Tragedy*, was the cause of Hieronymo's madness. It was Jessica who more cruelly struck the heart of Shylock with anguish. Jessica becomes the instrument for distraction, for determining this side of Shylock's character—that is, the distraught man, keen for vengeance at all costs and not willing to yield, almost maddened, grotesquely maddened, as Hieronymo became grotesquely maddened in the play of *The Spanish Tragedy*.

And notice—in some way or other both Marlowe and Shakespeare knew much about the Jews. How they knew it is difficult to tell, but they did know this : that your Jew may be in the public mind the vilest usurer. He may be as vile as may be. But there is one tender point, the sanctity of the home life. And it is marvellous, not so much with Shakespeare, because Shakespeare knew everything, but that Marlowe also knew this—that is the extraordinary part of it. As I said before, even as in *Romeo and Juliet*, seeing that the rivalry between the two houses demanded for their hatred the sacrifice of what is best and most lovable, namely, Romeo and Juliet—these two beautiful characters—so in this play of the other Italian city, Venice, Shakespeare sees the antagonism between the two castes, the caste of Shylock on the one hand and of the Christians on the other. He gives us a sort of minor counterpart, a minor play, a minor Romeo and Juliet—Jessica and Lorenzo.

It was not to be a tragedy, this play, but a tragi-comedy. How near to tears, how near to disaster ! For Shylock there was tragedy, though for the Elizabethan audience it made a comedy; so it is tragi-comedy. The tragi-comedy is cleverly brought about by Shakespeare through the desertion of Jessica and through nothing else. Up to that point Shylock did have the intention, according to Shakespeare, according to the Elizabethan audience hearing the play, of claiming this monstrous thing. But he would not have done so. The plea of mercy would have been too strong, the inherent human nature in the man was too strong till he became maddened, till he became distracted; and for that purpose Shakespeare gives this counterplot of Jessica and Lorenzo. But Shakespeare—this is another lesson that one is always learning as one tries to understand Shakespeare—the old idea that Shakespeare was an inspired rustic who wrote plays belongs to the past, at least I hope so—the idea that he was a clever dramatist even, that I hope belongs to the past—what people will understand more and more is this, that Shakespeare was *par excellence* a speaker, a thinker, a philosopher. That is what one has to bear in mind wherever one turns—from the early works to the crowning glory, *The Tempest* with its marvellous demand for music, where Shakespeare throws aside his magic garment, and drowns his book "deeper than did ever plummet sound." From the very beginning it is Shakespeare the thinker. He does nothing without thought, the great poet, the mighty poet, and he has chosen this medium for his poetry—people forget the Elizabethan stage and see the great platform stage. Shakespeare is the thinker; in *Romeo and Juliet* he speaks his own thoughts through such a humble character as the Friar, and the Friar comes in with a little flower —some flowers he had been collecting in an osier basket—and

sees wonder in this little flower. There is medicine and poison.
So in the human heart

> "Two such opposed kings encamp them still
> In man as well as herbs—grace, and rude will;
> And where the worser is predominant,
> Full soon the canker death eats up that plant."

And in this play, this play which has almost indirectly become
the counterpart of *Romeo and Juliet* from many points of view,
in this play where does the lesson come to us? Where? If I had to
say what is the burden of this play, this play that started as a mere
drama of usury, so clearly was it this and so clearly connected with
that idea I emphasised of Antonio standing really for the Christian
par excellence, himself—and Shylock, the hated Jew, for Evil,
and Portia, the Lady of Belmont, for Salvation—so clearly is this
so that I find a poet at the beginning of the seventeenth century
identifying Antonio with Christ. He played in his part upon the
mimic stage:

> "He died indeed, not as an actor dies,
> To die to-day, and live again to-morrow,
> In show to please the audience, or disguise
> The idle habit of enforcéd sorrow:
> > The Cross his stage was, and he played the part
> > Of one that for his friend did pawn his heart."

I say that incidentally all these things come in, yet all along
Shakespeare's mind is at work. He has used his character of
Shylock, the Cormorant, the Monster Cormorant. He uses him
not only as the Jew of Marlowe, the Hieronymo of *The Spanish*

32

Tragedy. Well, what of it? He argues the lesson we know, the great plea, "Hath not a Jew eyes, hath not a Jew hands." But after all, yet in spite of all, from the popular standpoint—and the Elizabethan only saw it from the popular Elizabethan standpoint, and it did not require a tragedy of Roderigo Lopez to embitter the popular mind against the Jew in Elizabethan times—what Shakespeare does is to think out the problem, and this is Shakespeare's own view of the whole subject. It is strange—the lesson of the play as Shakespeare sees it, namely, that man is what man has made him. The monster Shylock, this Cormorant, is what man has made of man. Only how true it is. We know that although the whole thing is a futile and monstrous legend, and that no Jew ever existed of the type of Shylock, we know that even if popular legend clung to that belief, popular legend made man to be such a monster as Shylock is—so Shakespeare did all this, even as he demanded the sacrifice of both Romeo and Juliet to the hatred of the rival houses, for to the prejudice of Shakespeare's time sacrifice means atonement for what is past.

The tragedy of the inner sacrifice of religion is often very clearly set forth. There must be the sacrifice before the atonement can be made; that is the attitude of tragedy in ancient Greece. It comes out in some of the teachings used by the Church at the very beginning and permeates the drama, when you have the Christian idea meeting with the old Greek demand for vengeance. But Shakespeare broods on the problem, and it is from the lips of Lorenzo, this minor Romeo, that the lesson of the play is enunciated. And notice this. It is spoken to the base and heartless Jessica, that almost light-of-love, who yet understands as truly as

33

Lorenzo the mystery and the wonder of it all. Beneath the starry night they sit and there the

> "Stillness and the night
> Become the touches of sweet harmony.
> Sit, Jessica. Look how the floor of heaven
> Is thick inlaid with patines of bright gold:
> There's not the smallest orb which thou behold'st
> But in his motion like an angel sings,
> Still quiring to the young-eyed cherubins;
> Such harmony is in immortal souls;
> But whilst this muddy vesture of decay
> Doth grossly close it in, we cannot hear it."

Yes, Lorenzo strikes the note. Shylock, too, has an immortal soul: the muddy vesture of decay is made more muddy by the scorn and the contempt of the Antonio of the time. There, too, is the music—if it could only be heard aright. And Shakespeare seems to emphasise that lesson to the Jessica who, after all, explains so much of the mystery, of the horror, of the monstrosity, of the character of Shylock. And Shakespeare perhaps seems to say "Yes: if, in popular prejudice, in the hatred of the mass of the people, this Shylock stands forth in harmony, in music as the jarring note of discord, yet he, too, is of the chosen." And to him, as Marlowe put it in the lips of his character, "came the promise."

And in Shakespeare's wisdom, perchance, Antonio's harmony and the music which he sounds might very well have been heard from Shylock himself, had not the world turned him into the pseudo-Cormorant we know him now to have been.

Shakespeare's "Shylock"
and
Scott's "Isaac of York"

From a lecture delivered before the Royal Institution
23rd April, 1920

When I was honoured by the request to address you this evening, it occurred to me that the occasion called, in the first instance, for some theme the treatment of which might, however inadequately, throw some new light on a Shakespearian problem, by way of due observance of Shakespeare Day; and, in the second place, the opportunity seemed to me a welcome one for recalling, in this place, that recently just one century has passed since the publication of perhaps the most popular of all Scott's novels, his romance of *Ivanhoe*. Accordingly, without wishing to attempt anything of the nature of a comparison of the genius of Shakespeare and Scott, I propose to submit to you certain considerations in respect of *The Merchant of Venice* and *Ivanhoe* that may perchance tend to deepen the understanding of the play, and cause us the better to appreciate how Scott endeavoured to redress in his novel what seemed to him to be difficulties well nigh insurmountable in the work of the great Master himself.

The soul of an artist is ever greater than his achievement; and the achievement is not only hampered by human limitations, but is affected in some measure by the timber or material or medium employed. And in attempting to understand the greatness of Shakespeare, one is forced to recognise that, however much he may transcend and transmute the rough timber on which he is working, integral elements of the material affect his treatment for good or bad. The myths and stories and old plays on which he worked represented different phases of development in story-lore, and these different phases stand for developments from different origins. In whatever rationalised form a nature myth or heroic myth may have come to Shakespeare to serve for the purposes of drama, the wonder of Shakespeare's genius may be seen in the manner in which he, all unconsciously, divined the germ of the myth. The rough, barbaric tale from which *Hamlet* emerged hid the far-off glory of a radiant spirit of Northern mythology, and Shakespeare's divining power invested the character anew with re-illumined significance. "The *Lear* of Shakespeare," said Lamb, "cannot be acted." Neither Shakespeare nor the critic studied folk-lore and origins. The rationalised story found in British history of the ancient British king and his three daughters gave no clue to its origin as derived from the myth of a Neptune-god with many turbulent daughters of the waves and one daughter gentle as a dove. But in Shakespeare's tempestuous play the Master reveals how his spirit has, all unbeknown to himself, rediscovered the integral germ of the history of Lear and his three daughters.

The Merchant of Venice presents difficulties which cannot be explained away by any preconceptions in respect of the predominant character of the play, Shylock. As one reads the play, one feels that Shakespeare's interest in this character from the human point of view is hampered and hindered by the plot, which in its main outline cannot be modified; it is just on this foundation-element of the story that the whole structure must be reared. Speciously as "a merry sport," but in reality with grim possibility of vengeance, Shylock induces the Merchant to be surety for his friend, a pound of his flesh to be the penalty in default of payment. Here lies the stumbling-block for the dramatist as for the actor. Such an unreal monster cannot be invested with the dignity with which Irving attempted to endow him, and the realism of a Moscovitch only deepens the unreality of the character in the earlier part of the play. It is easy enough to understand the distraught Shylock after Jessica's flight; the maddened and outraged father among the jeering Gentiles belongs to the realm of tragedy, and to a particular type of Elizabethan tragedy of vengeance, where a father or a son, smarting under a sense of wrong, becomes, through a phase of mental derangement, hardened in vengeful purpose that knows no yielding. But the "merry sport" of the bond, on which so much of the play depends, is a piece of grotesque unreality that conflicts with Shakespeare's attempt to portray a human character. Against these odds Shakespeare did his best for his Shylock,

"the red-haired Jew
Which sought the bankrupt merchant's pound of flesh,
By woman-lawyer caught in his own mesh."

In the old play on which Shakespeare must have worked, acted when he was still a school-boy at Stratford-on-Avon, the two main plots of *The Merchant of Venice* had already been combined, namely, the stories of "The Pound of Flesh" and "The Choice of the Caskets." I venture to submit that these two stories of *The Merchant of Venice* belong to the realm of parable, and not of reality; and I hold that this ultimate origin of the plot, all unbeknown, of course, to Shakespeare, enables us to understand certain problems of the play, and perhaps the fabric of the whole.

An endless number of analogues to both these stories is given in commentaries and studies on *The Merchant of Venice,* but both stories served, as investigation tends to prove, to exemplify Biblical texts; they were *exempla* or parables added to the texts for the purpose of vividly enforcing the meaning under a similitude. Such a medium of *exempla* as the famous *Gesta Romanorum,* which, indeed, contains some of the analogues of these two very stories, gives the best clue to their origin and purpose. Let me suggest the kind of text, perhaps the very texts themselves, that had these two stories as *exempla,* stories from which *The Merchant of Venice* was derived. "Greater love hath no man than this, that a man should lay down his life for his friend." "Christ also loved the Church (or Spouse) and gave Himself for it." From such texts as these came in due course the legend of "The Pound of Flesh" and "The Wooing of the Lady," which, through an earlier drama, became transmuted by Shakespeare into the play of *The Merchant of Venice.*

The merchant is willing to lay down his life for his *friend,* Bassanio, so that *he* (the friend, not he himself) may woo the lady, Salvation, the Spouse, the Bride, the heroic Portia. "To lay down his life for his friend." In an old English book of the thirteenth

38

century we read: "Do not men account him a good friend who layeth his pledge in Jewry to release his companion? Yea, God Almighty laid Himself in Jewry for us, and gave up His precious body to release His spouse out of the hands of the Jews. Never did friend give such a surety for his own friend." Hence medieval bias brings in the Jew with his bond, and the pledge suggests the problem of usury, and allows full play for racial and religious prejudice.

Readers of medieval literature are acquainted with the many allegories of the Four Daughters of God, found wide-spread in Latin, French, and English literature, originally evolved from *Psalm* lxxxv, 10: "Mercy and truth are met together, righteousness and peace have kissed one another." (In the old Aramaic: "Mercy and truth *thrust* at one another, justice and peace *fought together*.") There arose the allegory of the Four Daughters of God—Mercy and Truth, Justice and Peace—stating their various cases before the Deity, when He declared His intention to create man. This Hebrew parable passed through many developments, became in time Christianised, and Mercy *par excellence* became identified with Christian ethic. The medieval poem of *The Castle of Love* well attests the poetic possibilities of the parable. Portia, who pleads for mercy, was indeed not only, as I have indicated, the Church (or Spouse), but Mercy, one of God's Daughters herself; and the will of the dead father in respect of the caskets is really, in its ultimate origin, the will of the Heavenly Father. The successful wooer is he who makes choice of the leaden casket with the legend: "Who chooseth me must give and hazard all he hath." The other wooers are caught by the glamour of gold and silver, and fail in their quest. Bassanio, the friend, succeeds. All this, again, is vivid illustration of Scriptural texts on the value of earthly treasure.

I do not wish for a moment to suggest that anything of this was in Shakespeare's mind, but the drama of allegory was by no means dead in Shakespeare's time, and the medieval art of exposition by means of *exempla* was very near in kinship to actual allegory; and for those who are acquainted with the medieval drama, it does not require much effort to see Portia as Misericordia. Her plea for mercy epitomises, as it were, a whole moral play, and reveals the original significance of the Lady of Belmont.

Shakespeare does not call his play *The Jew of Venice,* but *The Merchant of Venice,* though the part of Antonio, important as it is in the story, is secondary in the drama. But a contemporary of Shakespeare, Joseph Fletcher, saw in the play something of what I am endeavouring to expound. Joseph Fletcher in his poem, *Christ's Bloodie Sweat,* 1613, wrote as follows:

"He died indeed, not as an actor dies,
　To die to-day, and live again to-morrow,
　In show to please the audience, or disguise
　The idle habit of enforcéd sorrow:
　　The Cross his stage was, and he played the part
　　Of one that for his friend did pawn his heart."

Elizabethan England was intensely interested in the problem of the taking of interest or usury, and although at that period there were practically no Jews in England (none were legally resident), yet naturally arising from the medieval stories underlying these two parables, usury is personified in the character of the Jew. It is a harsh character. True, Shakespeare endeavours to understand how, if man had been turned into such a creature, the fault is due to human contempt, hatred, the heaping up of ig-nominy, and all the degradations that those in ease, comfort, and freedom can inflict upon those denied the rights of humanity. In the play that Shakespeare used, as in *The Merchant of Venice,* the public saw the usurer in his worst light, still further darkened by religious animosities, due, not only to "theological odium," but also to the traditions of that earlier age, before the expulsion of Jews from England in 1290, hateful legends which inspired Chaucer's pathetic *Tale of the Prioress.* To give a Biblical veri-similitude to his play, Shakespeare has not only placed Biblical texts and a certain Biblical diction on the lips of Shylock, but the very names, Shylock, Tubal, Jessica, have their special significance, as in the case of so many of the names specially chosen for his characters by Shakespeare himself.

Schiloch is found, as the name of a Babylonian, in a famous Elizabethan rendering of the pseudo-Josephus. In the lists of Biblical Hebrew names with their explanations, often given at the end of the Bible, Shakespeare sought for likely names of his characters. Ingeniously he associated Schiloch with Shallach, the Biblical Hebrew for cormorant, the bird that swoops or dives after its prey. It came into the lists of Biblical animals, and so into glossaries, from *Leviticus* xi, 17, where it is mentioned among the forbidden fowls, to be held in abomination. In Elizabethan English, cormorant was an expressive synonym for "usurer," and perhaps the best commentary on the use of the word may be drawn from John Taylor's *Satires,* entitled "The Water-cormorant, his complaint against a brood of Land-cormorants," published in 1622. Shakespeare evidently knew the peculiar force of the words "to bait fish withal" uttered by his cormorant-usurer, the cormorant of the fictitious legend having its starting-point in the attempt vividly to exemplify the Biblical texts already quoted. The wealthy Hebrew of his tribe is called Tubal, a name not borne by Jews, and the name is given to the character, not with any suggestion of Tubal or Tubal Cain of *Genesis,* but because Tubal Cain was glossed in the Elizabethan books as meaning "worldly possessions, a bird's nest of the world."

He knew, too, why he chose Jessica, that is, Iscah, the daughter of Haran, as the name of Shylock's daughter. Elizabethans glossed the name as meaning "she that looketh out." She looked out beyond her father's home, and by her heartless defection goaded him to distraction. Shylock, who would not have parted with his Leah's turquoise ring for "a wilderness of monkeys," notwithstanding his maddened outcry in his first frenzy, would have given all his ducats for what was dearer to him, the daughter alienated from him by the attractions of the gay world outside the Ghetto walls. The Lorenzo and Jessica incident, a sort of minor Romeo and Juliet theme, does not in this play unite factions bitterly divided by causeless hate; it serves but to deepen and motivate the maddened sense of wrong that gives pathos to the character of Shylock. Yet it is under this sense of wrong that Shylock is made to utter his great plea at the bar of Humanity, and here it is that Shakespeare must have transcended the sentiments of his predecessor, as well as the motive underlying the whole story, which was to foster the spirit of intolerance and ill-will. To Jessica, the Juliet of the play, Lorenzo, a lesser Romeo, expounds the lofty doctrine of mystic harmony, the grander "music of the Cosmos":

> "Sit, Jessica. Look how the floor of heaven
> Is thick inlaid with patines of bright gold.
> There's not the smallest orb which thou behold'st
> But in his motion like an angel sings,
> Still quiring to the young-eyed cherubins;
> Such harmony is in immortal souls;
> But while this muddy vesture of decay
> Doth grossly close it in, we cannot hear it."

This is the real music of the play, the burden of Shakespeare's spirit, of Shakespeare the thinker, the myriad-minded, the humane, the wise, and the man of understanding, who looked forward hopefully to the allaying of the jarring notes that grate on the human soul.

Shakespeare's
"The Merchant of Venice"

(A Medievalist's Exposition)

Lecture at University College, Exeter
13th June, 1922

Mr. Principal, Ladies and Gentlemen—As the Principal has
already stated, this is the third time I have had the privilege of
addressing you in the capacity of Leofric Lecturer in this College.
And it may seem strange to some of you that whereas my duty is
to deal with Medievalism, I should have chosen to-day a subject
connected with the Elizabethan period, with Shakespeare himself
who, as we understand, transcends not only his own time, but all
time; and you may be wondering at my audacity in endeavouring
to link Shakespeare with the duties associated with the Leofric
Lectureship. No doubt the Chief of the Department here, Pro-
fessor Morgan, is also busy in his mind wondering whether I am
not rather bold and too audacious in this effort to justify my existence to-day. Well, in my first lecture I honourably adhered to my
duties in dealing with Old English poetry in the time of Leofric,
that poetry preserved so largely in the *Exeter Book*—that marvellous anthology of English literature before the Norman Conquest.
In my second lecture I attempted to demonstrate the place of the

45

Middle Ages—used in the most comprehensive sense of the term —in the lineage of English poetry. My effort in that lecture tended to demonstrate that the poetry of Langland and the school of West Midland poets that grew out of the Anglo-Saxon poems had their true place in the full development of English poetry right through the ages to our own time, and that those who attempted to nullify the worth of the old poetry were in many cases urging the plea through ignorance.

But in that lecture on the lineage of English poetry and the place the Middle Ages held in that progress, I said little indeed about Shakespeare. I merely hinted that even Shakespeare, belonging as he does to all time, but yet wearing as he did the apparel of his own age, showed unmistakably, in his going back to the medieval period for his plots, that the Elizabethan Age was *par excellence* the age when the Middle Ages met with the rediscovered Ages of Antiquity and were touched with the spirit of modern times. "The name is graven on the workmanship." That dictum is often thrust upon us by those who say: "Read your Shakespeare for himself; let your spirit apply itself to his work. Away with commentaries, away with studies of origins and sources of analogies; your dressing of timber is nothing; but the workmanship is everything. Bring your mind, or such mind as you may happen to have, to bear on the wonder of the finished piece of work."

But we are not all gifted as critics, even the best of us, fully to understand the finished piece of work. We may not have the right canons to apply for criticism. Our own efforts may be feeble, our intellect may not be able to soar to the poet's own height. And so,

46

as regards Shakespeare, large bodies of commentators and investi-
gators—men who have attempted to deal with origins—have been
at work for a good many years giving the materials for quickening
the appreciation of Shakespeare.

Take the case of those who have collected the origins of Shakespeare's work—the mere rough timber, it is true. They have pro-
vided excellent instruments for bringing home to people's minds
the difference between rough timber and the finished work. There
has been great value in their discoveries of the sources, origins,
and analogues of Shakespeare's plays. But while we have been
studying these origins and giving scholars and others useful instruments for quickening their appreciation, there has often
dawned upon us a feeling that it is possible to go farther back even
than origins, and enquire the source of these very origins. For
what is so remarkable about Shakespeare is that he often seems,
unconsciously to himself, to have divined the very germs of the
myths rationalised into authentic tale, history, and romance.

I will explain to you what I mean. Charles Lamb, one of the
most gifted and inspired of all our critics, said: "The *Lear* of
Shakespeare cannot be acted." But Shakespeare wrote his play and
presented his great figure of Lear to be acted. What did Lamb
mean? He meant there was something so tempestuous, so great,
so towering in the character, that our ordinary mimic stage could
not do justice, and no actor could do justice to it. Then comes
your student of origins. He points out that if you turn to early
British history, you will find the story of King Lear, an ancient
king of Britain, and his three daughters. Possibly it may be dramatised and produced in the Elizabethan Age. It is so. Later comes

your investigator into the origins of that British history, and what does he find? That Lear was originally a Neptune-god; that the turbulent daughters were the tumultuous waves, and that one of the daughters of this Neptune was a mild wave, gentle as a dove. The story as we have it in the British history is a rationalised nature myth, depicting a Neptune-god; and we understand how unconsciously in making his Lear so tempestuous, Shakespeare has caught, divined, as it were, unconsciously, the myth at the back of the rationalised types in ancient British legendary history. So the critic is justified: "The *Lear* of Shakespeare cannot be acted."

And so one might deal with *Hamlet,* and see Shakespeare taking the rude, barbaric tale of the North and so treating the characters, plucking out the heart of the mystery, as ultimately to give us the play which represents in some very vital way one of the noblest and most ancient of northern myths, where a young demi-god was, as it were, the Noonday Sun. And possibly Shakespeare's thought was, in those two cases I have mentioned, all unconscious of the real history of his legend, while in other cases possibly, and probably in his last play, *The Tempest*—his testament, as it were, to the world—he chose his story deliberately, in order to teach his own great lesson. He chose the myth with reference to some purpose that he had in his mind; some great lesson, that last phase of Shakespeare about which there has been so much discussion. In the Elizabethan Age there were poets, it is true; but we are thinking of how myths and stories may be used to point great lessons.

The story is of great interest wherever we turn in dealing with literature. We know how from ancient times—whether we turn to

Greece, whether we turn to India, or whether we turn (best of all) to ancient Judea—the story was used for teaching the lesson:

> "For Wisdom dealt with mortal powers
> Where Truth in closest words shall fail;
> When Truth embodied in a tale
> Shall enter in at lowly doors."

We know the purpose of the parable. We know that that method of allowing wisdom to enter in at lowly doors, through the tale, worked with wonderful effect right through the centuries until at last, by about the twelfth century, men of letters were busying themselves in collecting all possible tales they could find with reference to the enforcement of some lesson, some moral, some virtue, or some vice. The technical name given to the tale used for the purpose of enforcing some lesson was *exemplum*. A collection of *exempla* would form quite a library in any well-constituted medieval department of study. Throughout Europe collections were made in Latin, French, German, Italian and English, and especially Latin was used by writers in all countries so that their work might appeal to the general republic of scholars. Collections were made very often under alphabetical heads, or under texts, or under virtues, in order to illustrate the sermons, popular preachers finding it useless to talk in abstractions to their congregations. It was no use quoting texts with abstract qualities, with mere ideas. Even among the ancients, the great teachers taught thus: they all embroidered and emphasized their teaching by means of the most vivid stories *(exempla)* until, as some of you know, it became almost a source of annoyance to the great thinkers of the Middle

49

Ages when preachers brought in these stories, sometimes beneath the dignity of the Church. Dante expostulated against those who brought *Gesta* stories into their sermons. There are wonderful collections belonging to England. One of the mightiest of them has never yet been printed. It is by Bromyard, a contemporary of Wycliffe, who gives hundreds of stories, I suppose something like seven hundred, arranged under the heads of different virtues and vices, so that the preacher might easily find them. These *exempla* link themselves, of course, to Biblical teaching in the first instance. The parable was the great example of the *exemplum,* though if one were going into the matter in minute detail, one might differentiate between the parable as *exemplum* and other forms of tale.

Closely connected with the *exemplum* is, of course, allegory. It is about the twelfth century that we get allegory and mysticism introduced into modern literature in particularly close connection with narrative stories. I will take a passage from a book belonging to about the beginning of the thirteenth century because it will help to illustrate how I propose, as a medievalist, to bring home to you that in Shakespeare we have the essential elements of medieval legend, allegory, and mysticism—there will also be too often *odium theologicum*—and that these elements, which can be detected, could nevertheless, as far as Shakespeare himself is concerned, have been there quite unknown to him.

There is a book called *The Nuns' Rule.* I think it is one of the most beautiful books in English prose until we come to the writings of the great Elizabethans. It was written by a man who had a sense of humour, a sense of literature, and a sense of humanity.

He tells, under the section of Love, how there are different types of love : love between friend and friend; love between man and woman; love between mother and child; love between body and soul. The writer goes on to say : "The love which Jesus Christ hath to His dear Spouse surpasseth them all," and thus explains himself—"To this belongs a tale, and a lesson under cover of a similitude." And he tells a beautiful story : how there was once a lady who dwelt in a great castle, and how that castle was besieged, and how many princes came there. That none of them would help her until a great king, because of his love for her, came willing to give his life for her, and so drove away her foes. It is a story of the Christ wooing the human soul. And the writer goes on to say, after he has given this similitude : "Even so Christ gave Himself." Then comes an interesting passage : "Do not men account him a good friend who layeth his pledge in Jewry to release his companion? God Almighty laid Himself in Jewry for us, and gave up His precious body to release His spouse out of the hands of the Jews. Never did friend give such a surety for his own friend." The writer also says : "Christ so loved His spouse (the Holy Church) that He gave for her the price of Himself," and thus exemplifies the text of the Gospel : "Greater love hath no man than this, that a man lay down his life for his friend."

In the collections of *exempla* to which I have referred we have tales used in that definite way. Sometimes your tale is given by itself, the reader seeing obviously for what purpose the tale may be used. Sometimes moralising follows the tale, explaining what is meant by a whole allegory. Sometimes a Scripture tale precedes the *exemplum*. And sometimes you have a tale with a number of suggestive allegories following from the applications of the story and from different points of view. One of the greatest collections we have is the *Gesta Romanorum*. That is a collection of tales where after each tale a moralisation is given. In the *Gesta Romanorum* we have the story of the Pound of Flesh: how, in order to win the love of a lady—a rather fierce lady—a virago indeed—a certain young man borrows money from a man who is avaricious—a very monster. This monster is willing to lend money on condition that if it is not repaid by a certain day the young man shall forfeit one pound of his flesh. That story is explained in a moralisation: how the lady is the soul made in the likeness of God, and how the wicked monster is, of course, the Devil. That story we have in a great number of forms. Long before the *Gesta Romanorum* we have a form where the monster is closely bound up with the story of the Vision of the Cross, and the scene is transferred to the place where the Cross is found, and the monster is brought under the aegis of the Church. So the whole story has been softened down from the version that we have in the *Gesta Romanorum*.

Shakespeare did not take his story from the *Gesta Romanorum*. It came ultimately from Italy in the form of a romance. The romance or novella had nothing to do with allegory. Here was a good plot for a story, and the Italians made it into romance. It simply told the story with all the leading details which finally were used by some dramatist in England.

Why do I say *some* dramatist? Long before Shakespeare thought of dealing with the theme, when Shakespeare was still young—a schoolboy—the story of the Jew with reference to the same story that we have in Shakespeare's *Merchant of Venice* had been enacted on the English stage. As early as 1579 we have a reference to it, but the play is lost; we know it only from Gosson's reference. The man who dramatised that story did an extremely remarkable thing. He dealt not only with the story of the Pound of Flesh, but also with that other side of the story as we have it in Shakespeare, the Choice of the Caskets. This, too, is a story in the *Gesta Romanorum*. Not even in the *Gesta Romanorum* is it connected with the Pound of Flesh *exemplum*. It is entirely different, and belongs there to a different allegory, and a different homily. But there you have a choice; a lady making choice of the casket to win the hand of a prince. It is the woman who makes the choice of the casket, and not the man. We know at once, as we read that story of the Choice of the Casket in the *Gesta Romanorum,* that the young prince stands, of course, for Christ, and the human soul is the wooer.

In the story of the Pound of Flesh, as I indicated, the lady is a virago—a fierce, mercenary creature. All that had to be changed, and Shakespeare, or even the man who preceded Shakespeare, the dramatist I have alluded to, saw that some change was necessary, and introduced this other story, reversing the whole idea by making the man the wooer and the lady to be wooed. That is only another aspect of our allegory. Man, in the medieval times of mystical literature—man in his pilgrimage on earth—had to woo Grace Dieu, a noble lady, the daughter of the Divinity—Grace of God, as she was called, a noble and beautiful lady. A man walking on earth was qualified by his pilgrimage to be led ultimately to Grace Dieu—into the Divine Presence in his future life. In 1579 we have already two elements that make up *The Merchant of*

Venice; the Pound of Flesh motive on the one hand and, on the other, the Choice of the Caskets, combined into one play, *The Jew,* "representing the greedinesse of worldly chusers, and the bloody mindes of Usurers."

Let us look a little more closely into Shakespeare with reference to this lost play. I have said that the medieval preacher rightly caught hold of this idea of illustrating true wisdom by means of the tale, and driving it in until it entered at lowly doors. In the history of the drama the same thing took place. On the medieval stage you first had the dramatisation of the Biblical story, so that people might learn the story of Christ and the lives of the saints from these pageants. The teachers took the hint from this drama and said: "Why don't the dramatists use scriptural texts? Why not take your text from the Bible—your text so often replete with abstractions—and, supplying allegorical characters, let them act their parts." So there arose a second stage of medieval drama, the morality plays, which, dramatising abstractions, gave lessons for the betterment of human life. As we come to the Elizabethan period, these morality plays, though still written and acted, very often combine with abstractions real characters; and there can be little doubt, I think, that the play of *The Jew,* as acted in 1579 when Shakespeare was a boy, represented Lucre and Covetousness and Want of Conscience, and that, later, combined with these abstractions were real characters—the Jew on the one hand, and some of those other characters, the prototypes of Shakespeare's characters. It comes as a surprise to students to discover that while Shakespeare was writing some of his greatest plays of the early period, dramatists were still writing morality plays. The morality plays were still being acted and being printed for the delectation of the people. Indeed, the author of a similar play which would have been valuable to us to illustrate my theme was a member of such a company, and was afterwards in Shakespeare's own company. His name was Robert Wilson, an interesting figure.

Let us "watch" Shakespeare's play. Regard me for the moment as being a medievalist approaching the matter from his own standpoint. Arising from your two *exempla,* you have your Antonio, your good friend, your perfect friend, a man who is very carefully described as the dearest friend, and you remember how the term "friend" is used theologically and with what fine effect. He is

> "The dearest friend—the kindest man,
>   The best condition'd and unwearied spirit
>   In doing courtesies."

There is Bassanio on his pilgrimage to woo the lady. Think of the lady in Belmont

>   "richly left;
>   And she is fair, and fairer than that word,
>   Of wondrous virtues . . .
>   Her name is Portia; nothing undervalued
>   To Cato's daughter, Brutus' Portia :
>   Nor is the wide world ignorant of her worth;
>   For the four winds blow in from every coast
>   Renowned suitors."

Yea, they come from all Europe, France and Germany and far-off America, wooing this fair lady Grace Dieu. And Bassanio comes

55

too, and Antonio, the perfect friend, so passive, so quiet, and yet destined to give his name to the whole play.

And Bassanio! I can imagine some of you saying: "Well, it was not an ideal thing to get his friend to borrow money for him that he might make a great show to win this noble heiress!" But when the test came, Bassanio stood the test. He, too, would have been willing to give himself if he could to have rescued his friend, willing to give wife and all. But you will say: "Why, if this man was ultimately to make choice of the leaden casket, as though he didn't care about the vain glories of the world, why borrow three thousand ducats under such conditions, and why go pranked out in clothes that really were not his?" But would you have a man enter on his quest for a noble lady, as it were for the divine Grace Dieu, in clothes beflecked with mire, unfit to enter so noble a presence? Think of your parable of the wedding feast. And so, too, of Portia. Look at her environment, her noble palace, all the beauty and charm of high life about her. Grace Dieu. Yea, do not all the great philosophers and teachers tell us, whether we turn to the Bible or turn to the Greek, that with truth and wisdom are two other aspects of beauty—charm and grace? The palace above, the heavenly mansion, must have something resembling it for the Grace Dieu on earth.

Indeed, I am making this suggestion to some of you that Shakespeare's Bassanio, in his quest for Portia, has points of contact with Spenser's Red Cross Knight in search of Una. They are not absolutely different. Your Knight of Holiness, it is true, must wear the armour of holiness, of truth and goodness, must climb the great hill and catch a glimpse of the heavenly Jerusalem, that

56

he may the better thereafter "fight the good fight." Yes, that is one type. But your man of the world must also win his Portia, even though he must prank himself out in worldly garments; must do his best to win her.

The test came with the caskets. What is the meaning of the test? You remember the text in the Bible: "Your gold and silver is cankered; and the rust of them shall be a witness against you." Make an *exemplum* of that, and you have your caskets. The ideal for winning Grace Dieu was to ignore gold and silver, the empty pomp and show, and to choose that which was inscribed: "Who chooseth me must give and hazard all he hath." Bassanio proves that he was justified in attempting to win the hand of Portia, for ultimately, as I said, he stood the test and would have hazarded all to save his friend, if he could. That resembles Antonio. Though when, as you may remember, it is said by Portia of Antonio,

> "this Antonio,
> Being the bosom lover of my lord,
> Must needs be like my lord,"

your medieval point of view would have been the other way round; what is called the doctrine of imitation: conform yourself to pattern. Though Portia, seeing Bassanio, her beloved one, as the most glorious man, actually says, "Antonio, being the bosom lover of my lord, must needs be like my lord," your medievalist understanding was at the back of it. The old *exemplum* usage would have put it the other way: "This Bassanio, being such a friend, must needs be like his friend." Now we have our Antonio, our Bassanio, and we have our Portia.

57

As I noted earlier, in the *Gesta Romanorum* the monster who exacts, or is wishing to exact, the pledge is the Evil One—I mean the devil. The medieval theology, as I said, the *odium theologicum*, linked the matter directly, and turned this monster into a Shylock against whose race popular prejudice throughout all ages had deepened and deepened until the time that Chaucer gave to that object the cruel legend of *The Prioress's Tale*:

> "Oure firste foo, the serpent Sathanas,
> That hath in Jewes herte his waspes nest."

But if you look at the theological point of view, you see exactly how the figure stands for Shylock, and that brings me to Shakespeare's real problem.

The pledge of the pound of flesh was to be exacted by Shylock as a mere afterthought. A merry idea seems to have occurred, as it were, Shylock saying that if Antonio did not pay his pledge, the pound of flesh should be the payment. Shakespeare, getting as far as that in doing his work, came to a difficulty. The whole thing gave him great difficulty. After all, no man ever in real life demanded such a pledge. It belongs not to nature, not even to myth, but rather to farce. It would have done very well for farce, or indeed for real tragedy if certain elements were there to deepen the matter; but Shakespeare's play was a blend of tragedy and comedy, his first great experiment in tragi-comedy. As he dealt with his subject the theme fascinated him. The humanity of the problem appealed to him. He saw that this element of the story, the integral element, the pound of flesh, could not be got rid of; he saw that although that element was unnatural and improbable, yet the character of Shylock was a character representing tragedy —the tragedy of humanity, the tragedy of race, and the tragedy of religion. The theme fascinated him more and more. He put into Shylock's mouth that great plea uttered at the bar of humanity that differentiated Shakespeare so much from any predecessor in drama; and to a large extent (not altogether) from writers of the Middle Ages. It was not that he held a brief for Shylock, but that the problem appealed to him; and I hold, with a very perfect faith, that great as Shakespeare is as a dramatist, great as he may be as a poet, greater still is he as a thinker. Primarily, Shakespeare is a man who is a philosopher; who allows his wisdom and his view of life to speak, not in his case through *exemplum,* but through dramatic form from the platform stage—which rightly was called the platform stage. It was the platform where he enunciated so many of his thoughts. Uttering that plea was not enough for the purposes of drama; though it would do for the pamphleteer, the man holding a brief. The dramatic necessity for Shakespeare was to deal with his character so as to account for it. For that purpose he created an underplot.

Naturally we come to that underplot of Jessica and Lorenzo in *The Merchant of Venice.* Until we come to that, the whole problem of Shylock is difficult, and we find that Shakespeare is troubled as to how to treat the thing. By means of Jessica, the character and purpose of Shylock are to be so intensified as to give probability. No longer are we in doubt as to whether any monster can possibly, under any condition, exact such a pledge. Through Jessica, those who have been most scornful of Shylock are now put in position to triumph over him until the man becomes obsessed, his character deepened and maddened with the idea of carrying through his purpose. His is an obsession not just of the tragedy of vengeance, but of a particular type of tragedy—that other drama of vengeance best exemplified by *The Spanish Tragedy*, where a man has suffered wrong, and is so obsessed with the idea of vengeance as to become maddened and lose all sense of reason. One idea obsessed him. That obsession in tragedy ends in death and disaster; for the man, the hero, who is thus maddened, not only deals vengeance to those who have wronged him, but kills himself also. But Shakespeare's play had to be tragi-comedy. We have now, therefore, got Shakespeare dealing with his two-fold subject, the pound of flesh and the choice of the casket, and also this underplot of Jessica and Lorenzo.

Turn to the audience listening to the play. What was the theme that struck them most vividly? It was the figure of Shylock as the usurer incarnate. The play was a lesson to them, primarily a play dealing with the problem of usury; and Shylock was the embodiment of usury, as in the medieval morality play you have the character of Lucre, or usury. I would like to say a word about Shylock as the embodiment of usury. How came it that in the Middle Ages usury was so strongly condemned and, perhaps, rightly? The condemnation of it belongs to the interpretation of the passage in *Luke,* the famous passage you know very well: "But love ye your enemies, and do good, and lend, hoping for nothing again." Here is the way it was interpreted: "nihil inde sperantes"—"lend your money hoping for nothing in return." I make the rendering of "nihil inde sperantes" to be "never despairing of any hope for anything." But the canon law of the

Middle Ages insisted on the interpretation, "You must lend and take no interest." They excommunicated those that transgressed the canon law. It was very hard in some cases, especially when the civil powers wished to raise a good deal of money. The only way then was to get the Jews, who could not well be excommunicated, to do what could not be done under the conditions of canon law; and so this people were forced throughout the Middle Ages to practise usury, and nowhere had a chance of taking up any other calling. They were to carry out what canon law considered as evil and as deserving excommunication. Civil law therefore stepped in, in the position of ruler—lord or king—and took the Jews under its protection; took also a fair share of the high interest they were allowed to exact. But in England from 1290 right up to Cromwell, Jews were not resident in England, and therefore Shakespeare, in dealing with Shylock, was dealing with medieval tradition in an extremely interesting way. In his time the general discussion was whether ordinary folk should lend money. There was a great deal of usury going on in Shakespeare's time, and it was not supposed to be so very bad. There was one neighbour of Shakespeare whose mock epitaph was:

> "Ten in the hundred lies here ingrav'd;
> 'Tis one hundred to ten his soul is not sav'd:
> If any man ask, 'who lies in this tomb?'
> 'Oh! ho!' quoth the Devil, ''tis my John-a-Combe.'"

John Combe was a great friend who left Shakespeare a sum of money in his will.

Shakespeare got so interested in the subject when he was dealing with it that he said to himself : "This man, this Shylock, this problem of the Jew; what about these people?" Then it occurred to Shakespeare, who was an ardent reader of the Bible and knew it from cover to cover, to look further into this race that brought forth the prophets. He touched the whole speech of Shylock with almost Biblical idiom. He did more than that. The name of Shylock has been a problem for a long time. Why should he be called Shylock? It occurred to me that Shakespeare had turned to the end of the Bible where the names in the Bible and their explanations are given, as we find in old Bibles going back to the Middle Ages when men were fond of etymology. There was one creature forbidden in *Leviticus* to be eaten by the Jews—the cormorant; in Hebrew: *shallach;* but "cormorant" to Elizabethans meant usurer in the same way that we use the term "vampire." Shakespeare, reading an interesting history where a ruler called Shiloch is mentioned, links the name of Shiloch with shallach, the name of the cormorant, and there you have the figure of the cormorant putting his beak right down into the water to catch little fishes.

It is only a little while ago that I discovered another clue to show how Shakespeare was a student as well as a philosopher and a dramatist. Why should the friend of Shylock be called Tubal? It is not a name borne by Jews, and neither Tubal nor Tubal Cain of *Genesis* seems at all an appropriate name for the companion of the Jew of Venice. But Tubal Cain was glossed in Elizabethan commentaries on the Bible as meaning "worldly possessions, a bird's nest of the world," hence Tubal, the wealthy Hebrew of the tribe.

I would like to say a word or two about Jessica. That was

Shakespeare's great discovery, I think. Jessica is the Elizabethan form of Iscah, the name of the daughter of Haran in *Genesis*. It is glossed in those dictionaries: "She that looketh out." She looked out from the narrow Ghetto; from the casement of her house she looked into the open world, the world outside the Ghetto. It is wonderful how Shakespeare has worked in the underlying etymology of the name. She looks out of the casement although her father has told her not to watch for the aliens, for those painted fellows coming along, those Gentile masqueraders, lest she be caught by them and see the narrowness of imprisonment. She does look out beyond her father's home, and by her heartless defection she goads him to distraction. In Jessica and Lorenzo Shakespeare gives us an underplot corresponding to *Romeo and Juliet*. Even as in *Romeo and Juliet* he had shown what the results were when hatred divides the families of one great town—the canker of death eats up the blossom—so here, dealing again with a great Italian city, he shows what happens where hatred divides people through race and religion. Of his lesser Romeo and Juliet in this play, of Jessica and Lorenzo, I shall speak in a moment.

Let us first come to the Trial scene. That, to my mind, is a problem which has not received proper attention. Shakespeare saw the difficulty. You have your Trial scene. And what a Trial scene it is! Your Portia seems at one time Mercy, at another time Justice. What is your Duke who is at the head of the Tribunal? Jurists have written a great deal about the law of the Trial scene as though Shakespeare wished to give the impression of a Royal Court of Justice. Now one of the earliest commentators who wrote on the subject of the Trial scene was a gentleman of Exeter. In

1792, in a collection of essays, he dealt with the theme in an extraordinarily interesting way. He said that centuries hence Shakespeare would be spoken of as the "ancient British Bard," and the *Jerusalem Gazette* would publish an account of the Hebrew *Merchant of Venice,* and he went on to dwell, as a critic of that time, on the Trial scene. That gentleman of Exeter had interesting points in mind, and there is a great deal of truth in his *jeu d'esprit.*

What is the Trial scene in *The Merchant of Venice?* For that I must take you back again to medievalism. There was one interesting Psalm that of all others affected commentators from the earliest times. It was the 85th Psalm, the Psalm that belonged to Christmas Day; telling of the time when there should be great glory in the world—when mercy and truth should meet together, and righteousness and peace should kiss each other; when truth was to spring out of the earth, and righteousness to look down from heaven. The early commentators said: "Who are these people—Mercy and Truth and Righteousness and Peace?" They personified them. They made them first of all attributes of God —the four daughters of God. They made out a wonderful story: how man transgressed at the Fall through disobedience, and the four daughters of God—Mercy, Truth, Righteousness and Peace —came before Him. Mercy said: "Spare him; do not let your fiat go forth." Truth said: "Yea, but he hath sinned." Righteousness, or Justice, said: "He must be punished." And Peace said: "Let us see whether we cannot harmonise all these elements together." We see them in the twelfth century, when the whole literature of mysticism was growing up, and later in the French drama we have these figures introduced. The English drama has them. In some French morality plays we have a whole scene devoted to this pleading. One version was called the *Processus Belial,* which later was transferred to the mystery play of the *Passion,* and then influenced the trial of Antonio on the one hand, and Shylock on the other. The problem of Mercy and Justice for all mankind grew out of the medieval dramatising of this idea; the mysticism associated with the wonderful medieval allegory of *The Four Daughters of God.* In Mercy and Justice are those sisters reconciled and harmonised. Medieval theology can justify it.

And Shakespeare failed not. He felt there was something amiss in the plot before him. Righteousness and Peace have not kissed. We come to the last Act of *The Merchant of Venice.* There we have Shakespeare's personality coming out abundantly. Supposing the play had ended with the Trial scene. How unsatisfactory it would have been! Nothing could have been more unsatisfactory. Mercy and Justice would not have harmonised.

In the fifth act, through two minor characters of the play, and, perchance, where we would least expect it, through Lorenzo and Jessica, Shakespeare speaks, and transmutes everything in the play up to that point into his own wonderful golden work. Shakespeare often speaks through a minor character. In *Romeo and Juliet,* through the Friar he taught his lesson. He allowed the Friar to come in with a basket of herbs, to take up one herb and say:

"Within the infant rind of this small flower
Poison hath residence, and medicine power:
For this, being smelt, with that part cheers each part,
Being tasted, slays all senses with the heart."

65

And so within the human heart,

> "Two such opposed kings encamp them still
> In man as well as herbs—grace, and rude will."

What was the lesson to be learnt here? Jessica and Lorenzo
were not introduced in order to satisfy the requirement: a sacrifice
to hatred—and thus divide their religion and race. That was not
to be the lesson, but another lesson more marvellous than that of
Romeo and Juliet. Lorenzo, with gay spirit and youthful, is
talking to Jessica; and suddenly we hear pronounced the theory
of the heavenly spheres, the music of the universe. Could anything
be more marvellous than that? He to Jessica, the daughter of
Shylock, uttered these immortal words:

> "Sit, Jessica. Look how the floor of heaven
> Is thick inlaid with patines of bright gold:
> There's not the smallest orb which thou behold'st
> But in his motion like an angel sings,
> Still quiring to the young-eyed cherubins;
> Such harmony is in immortal souls;
> But while this muddy vesture of decay
> Doth grossly close it in, we cannot hear it."

"Such harmony is in immortal souls." Medieval people are
they, going right back to Antiquity—because the doctrine of the
heavenly spheres came right through the Middle Ages down to
the Renaissance. Plato's *Timaeus* we know through the Latin
translation of the fourth century. Shakespeare thought of the
wonderful idea of the world moving to music; that in each human

66

heart there is some music; that only those pure of heart—away from the evil of the world, away from the muddy vesture of decay —can catch the heavenly music; but while this muddy vesture closes it in, we cannot hear it. We cannot hear the music in our hearts corresponding to the music of the spheres, and we cannot hear the music in other men's hearts; we cannot hear the music in their souls where misery, where contempt, where injustice, where hatred, make the human soul, as it were, a noble thing placed in a tenement corroded over, even as iron chains corrode. "As fetters corrode the flesh, so persecution corrodes the heart." As man does to man, so persecution and contempt do to the human soul. They place the human soul in a veritable corroded thraldom; we cannot hear the music of such a one, and we cannot hear our own.

That theory of the music of the spheres goes back to the mysticism of the Middle Ages in a remarkable way. Shakespeare does not borrow the whole thing from Plato directly or indirectly. He links the Platonic idea with the Biblical, and in place of the Sirens in Plato we have the Cherubim. That he derives from the medieval plays; "Seraphim" was the word the prophet Isaiah used. The idea of the music of the spheres we have in Pythagoras; and Plato uses this in a remarkable way. Then we have it declared in *Job* that "the morning stars sang together." The medieval idea of the mystics was very wonderful. It was this: that souls away from the uncleanliness of the world may catch the echo, an echo, as it were, of the heavenly music.

The idea was very beautiful. And Shakespeare, through the speech of Jessica and Lorenzo, in a marvellous way shows us his hope that man divested of all the muddy vesture—which is not merely the corporeal flesh, but evil, that is, hatred, indignity, narrowness, strife—all those elements removed, may then have hope again. Then it is as though Shakespeare had this idea: Truth will spring up from the earth; and Righteousness will meet Truth from heaven; Mercy and Truth will meet together; and Righteousness and Peace will kiss. So the whole of that play is rounded off with the idea that fascinated Shakespeare: the problem of harmony.